The Butterfly

This book has been reviewed
for accuracy by

Eugene L. Lange, Ph.D.
Assistant Professor of Zoology
University of Wisconsin—Milwaukee

Library of Congress Number: 78-26827

10 11 12 13 14 15 16 17   W   99 98 97 96 95 94 93 92

Library of Congress Cataloging in Publication Data

Hogan, Paula Z
  The butterfly.

  Cover title: The life cycle of the butterfly.
  SUMMARY: Describes the physical characteristics and
the life cycle of the butterfly.
  1. Butterflies—Juvenile literature. [1. Butterflies]
I. Strigenz, Geri K. II. Title. III. Title: The
life cycle of the butterfly.
QL565.2.H63 595.7'89 78-26827
ISBN 0-8172-1252-3 hardcover library binding
ISBN 0-8114-8176-X softcover binding

The
BUTTERFLY

By Paula Z. Hogan
Illustrations by Geri K. Strigenz

RSVP
RAINTREE
STECK-VAUGHN
P U B L I S H E R S
The Steck-Vaughn Company

 # The Butterfly

High on a hill, there are two butterflies. They are called monarchs. The male moves his wings up and down. A mating smell comes from spots on his wings.

The female has a mating smell also. The two butterflies land on a leaf and mate.

8

Soon the female flies off. She looks for a place to lay her eggs. Monarchs lay their eggs on the leaves of the milkweed plant.

After three or four days, a caterpillar hatches. First it eats its egg shell. Then it eats leaves. Birds sometimes eat caterpillars. But these caterpillars taste bad.

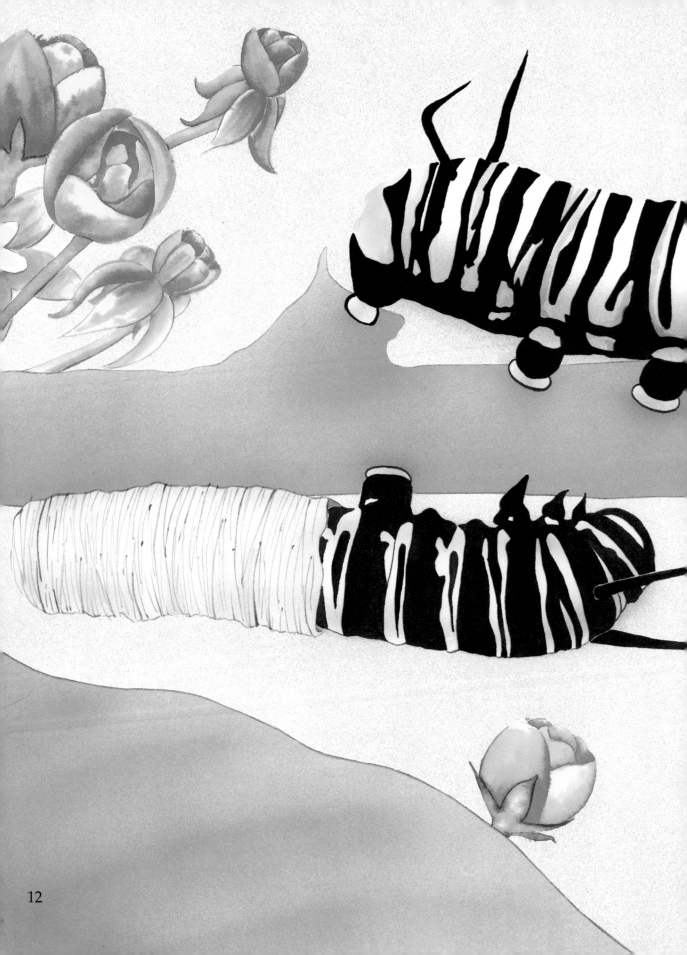

Soon the caterpillar grows too large for its skin. The old skin splits open. Under it is a bigger one. This happens several times.

After two weeks, the skin splits
again. The caterpillar changes into
a pupa. The pupa forms a
chrysalis. It has tiny holes in it to
let air in and out. The pupa inside
grows into a butterfly.

After two weeks, the chrysalis breaks open. Out comes a butterfly. At first, its wings are wet and crushed. Soon the sun dries them.

The butterfly does not eat
leaves. It gets food from flowers.
When the butterfly is not eating,
its mouth parts are rolled up.

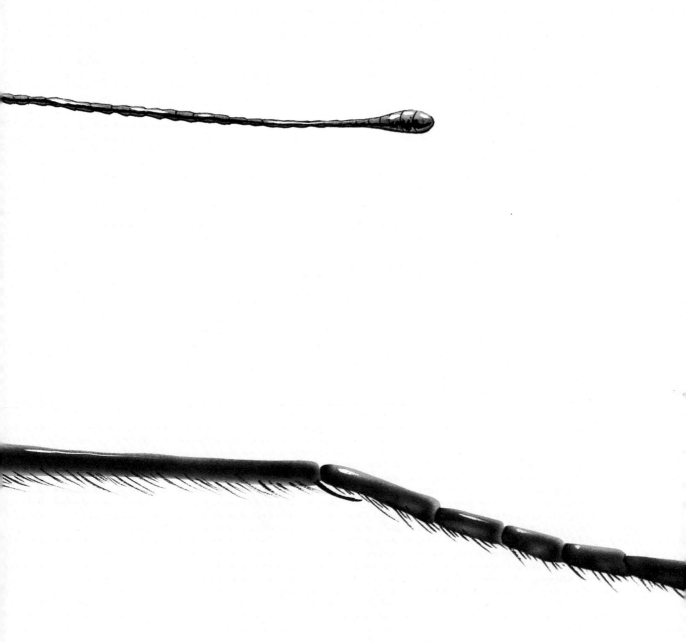

The butterfly tastes with its feet.
On its head are two antennae. The
butterfly smells with the antennae.

Most butterflies fly only on sunny days. On each side of its body are two wings. The back and front wings are linked together by tiny hooks.

close-up of scales

Tiny colored scales cover the wings. Bright colors warn birds to keep away. The butterflies taste bad too!

Monarch butterflies live where it is warm. When it gets cold, they fly away to where it is warmer.

In spring, the butterflies start to
fly back. On their way, they stop
to lay eggs. The butterflies that are
born follow the others.

chalk-hill blue butterfly

Butterflies live all over the world. The chalk-hill blue butterfly is found in England. Glasswing butterflies live in Central American rain forests. The painted lady butterfly is found in many parts of the world.

glasswing butterfly

painted lady butterfly

GLOSSARY

These words are explained the way they are used in this book. Words of more than one syllable are in parentheses. The heavy type shows which syllable is stressed.

antennae (an·**ten**·nae)—long feelers on a butterfly's head

caterpillar (**cat**·er·pil·lar)—a furry worm that changes into a pupa, then a butterfly

chalk-hill blue—butterfly that lives in England and is usually blue

chrysalis (**chrys**·a·lis)—a covering

glasswing (**glass**·wing)—Central American butterfly whose wings are almost clear

hatches (**hatch**·es)—eggs opening to let caterpillars out

mating smell (**mat**·ing smell)—what a butterfly smells like before it joins together with its mate

milkweed (**milk**·weed)—plant with sticky juice in its stems

monarch butterfly (**mon**·arch **but**·ter·fly)—an American black and orange butterfly

painted lady (**paint**·ed **la**·dy)—a brown and orange butterfly

pupa (**pu**·pa)—a caterpillar, inside a chrysalis, before it changes into a butterfly

scales—small thin coverings